ZENCOLOR BLOOMS

An Adult Spring Coloring Book

ANGE MARIE DWYER

© 2017 by Painted Grace Books

Illustrations © 2017 Angela Marie Dwyer
Text © 2017 Angela Marie Dwyer

First published in the United States of America in 2017 by
Painted Grace LLC, dba
Painted Grace Books
Colorado Springs, CO 80916
www.paintedgrace.com
Visit www.paintedgrace.com for a behind the scenes look at the artist, design process and other products.

All rights reserved. No part of this book may be reproduced in any form without written permission of the copyright owners. All images in this book have been reproduced with the knowledge and licensed consent of the artists concerned, and no responsibility is accepted by the producer, publisher, or printer for any infringement of copyright or otherwise, arising from the contents of this publication. Every effort has been made to sensure that credits accurately comply with information supplied and licenses required. We apologize for any inaccuracies that may have occured and will resolve inaccurate or missing information in any subsequent reprinting of the book.

ISBN-13: 978-1543290394
ISBN-10: 1543290396

Digital edition: unvailable

Design: Painted Grace Studios

Printed in the United States of America

INTRODUCTION

Years ago, I was sitting at my local bookshop with one of my best friends musing about an idea of an adult style coloring book. I never got around to finishing mine but imagine my surprise to see lots of other wonderful artists had the same idea. What an explosion adult coloring books have become!!!

I remember the joy the simple act of coloring brought me as a child and I hope you find the same sense of peace and happiness that I did. We are faced with responsibilities and hardships that can wreak havoc on our minds, bodies, and souls. These spring-inspired illustrations are images to help you spark your creative side while providing you with hours of fun, entertainment and stress relief.

You will find pages filled with drawings, ranging from simple to detailed that feature flowers, bunnies, hanging birdcages, butterflies, leaves and more that will bring the hope and beauty of spring into your life and soul no matter where you are and what kind of day you're having.

And for you, the creative colorist, I tried to ensure that there was plenty of border room so that you can either doodle along the edges or cut out your colorful page to display on your wall, or maybe to wrap a small present or even, make the most colorful paper airplane ever!

Before you begin coloring, feel free to use a couple of pages at the beginning of the book to test out your supplies for color, smoothness, bleed thru etc...
Enjoy taking some time for yourself!

xoxo xoxo,

Ange Marie

These pages are for you!
You can DOODLE or TEST YOUR PENS here.

www.ingramcontent.com/pod-product-compliance
Lightning Source LLC
LaVergne TN
LVHW081209050225
803024LV00014B/1140